"Advanced" Fairy Tales on Trial

by Janis L. Silverman

Cover by Greg Lawhun
Graphic Production by Pamela Pirk
© 2000 Pieces of Learning
1990 Market Road
Marion IL
polmarion@midamer.net
www.piecesoflearning.com
CLC0235
ISBN 1-880505-73-8
Printing No. 54321
Printed in the U.S.A.

Table of Contents

WHO NEEDS THIS BOOK?

All classroom teachers, enrichment coordinators, teachers of gifted and talented, and students will enjoy the experiences in *"Advanced" Fairy Tales on Trial* as a vehicle to teach Character Education through critical thinking and problem solving.

The trials teach children to analyze values and character in the lives of others as well as in their own lives within the framework of the judicial process. The simulated trials present a forum for teamwork using a challenging and creative process.

FROM THE AUTHOR

Prior to entering school, students learn values and "rules" at home. Their second learning front is at school where students learn acceptable behaviors in cooperating, working and playing with others. Teachers try to prepare students for the world in which they live in various ways. When students see how behavior connects to the standards of society, they gain an understanding of the laws and the standards which govern our society.

My purpose in writing *"Advanced" Fairy Tales on Trial* is to provide a framework for students in which to experience the process of a trial and all of the critical thinking that accompanies the preparation of a case. Students will read fairy tales with a critical eye, assessing the behaviors of the characters. They will determine whether or not a character should be charged and tried for a crime. If a fairy tale character goes to trial for a crime, the class will be involved in preparing all of the necessary elements of the trial. They will develop legal arguments, opening and closing statements, and questions for the witnesses. Finally, the class will present the case to another class, who serves as the jury.

Critical reading, critical thinking, point of view, persuasive and analytical writing, drama, cooperation, and teamwork are skills that will develop through the work of a fairy tale trial. The feedback and assessments I have done with classes who have completed fairy tale trials show that students were challenged throughout the process. The jury deliberation has been an intriguing process. Students will grasp an understanding of the laws governing behaviors in our society through preparing and enacting these trials.

Fairy tales are the vehicle for authentic learning and create a real connection between the world of children and the greater society in which they live. I have used fairy tale trials to add a new dimension to language arts. I have seen students integrate all of their language arts skills and draw upon their critical thinking skills. They have thought and acted like a lawyer or experienced a trial as a witness or a member of a jury. What an exciting process this is!

You are about to lead or facilitate a challenging and exciting set of experiences for your students. You will help your students apply their language arts and thinking skills as lawyers, judges, witnesses or defendants in criminal court cases. This is authentic learning at its best. Please note that the length of the sessions that follow will vary depending upon the age and sophistication of your students. Note that although some fairy tales' endings have already "eliminated" characters, proceed with trials as if those characters are still alive. Use the form on page 64 to assess students.

In using *"Advanced" Fairy Tales on Trial*, fairy tale cases need not be listed by suggested grade level. Any one of the cases in this book is suitable for grades three through nine. When a defendant can be charged with more than one "count" or charge, such as the soldier in the *Tinder Box*, the complexity of the case can be simplified by presenting a trial with only one count. Choose a case by the content of the story, the character issues raised, its literary appeal to your students, the charges against the defendant, and the level of challenge you'd like to offer your students. To create more challenge, let the students evaluate a case and come up with their own list of charges.

A few fairy tales could actualize into more than one fairy tale trial. For example, the *Tinder Box* could result in a trial of the King and Queen vs the Soldier or in the trial of the Witch vs the Soldier because the soldier could be charged with criminal behavior by more than one person. Note the heading on Pretrial Discussion Question pages for more than one suggested trial per fairy tale.

Cases and Related Issues:

Little Red Riding Hood . . . . greed, deceit, tricking another, safety, don't talk to strangers

The Tinder Box . . . . honesty, trust, choices, money & power, rule by fear

Sleeping Beauty . . . . jealousy, envy, revenge, choices

Toads and Diamonds . . . . . kindness and generosity are rewarded; selfishness is not; manners

The Bremen Town Musicians . . . . Does desperation and suffering justify breaking the law?

The Hare and the Hedgehog . . . . deceit, prejudice, cruelty, diversity, tolerance

Aladdin and the Wonderful Lamp . . . . Does money buy happiness? Success?, deceit

The Gingerbread Man . . . . honesty, deceit, independence, choices

The Pied Piper of Hamelin . honesty, deceit, laziness, problem solving, threatening others

Cinderella . . . . family, love and acceptance, ridicule, harassment

Two Bad Mice . . . . retribution, protection of one's property, personal responsibility

SESSION ONE: WHERE TO BEGIN

1. Begin with the following PRETRIAL CLASS DISCUSSION QUESTIONS to help prepare your class for a fairy tale trial.

PRETRIAL CLASS DISCUSSION QUESTIONS

(A) Why do we have laws?

(B) What laws do you know about?

(C) How do our laws protect us?

(D) What happens when someone breaks a law?

(E) Are all crimes the same? Which crimes are more serious than others? Why?

(F) Is every wrongdoing solved by a trial in a court? Explain.

(G) Which behaviors are not solved by a trial?

(H) Why do we have trials?

(I) What questions do you have about laws? trials?

2. Prepare *Student Information Packets, Jury Packets,* and *Lawyer Packets* by copying appropriate student pages. See page 8.

3. Refer to the *Criminal Behavior Chart* on pages 9-10 to help students understand what constitutes *criminal* behavior.

4. Use the *Glossary of Legal Terms* on pages 62-63 in your discussion with the students.

5. Explain the roles of the defense and prosecuting lawyers, the judge, the bailiff, the defendant, the witnesses, and the jury. Refer to the *Trial Roles* on pages 14-16. Answer any of the questions the students may have at this time.

1. Choose a fairy tale from the list. Copy and read the introductory page about the particular tale to introduce the case to the students.

2. Obtain the original fairy tale from your learning center or library. Read the tale in its entirety.

3. Ask the students to think about and analyze the behaviors of the characters in the fairy tale. The students will write their ideas about these characters' behaviors explaining why they thought a character's behavior was "acceptable" or "unacceptable." Guide the students, individually, in small groups, or as a class, in filling out the *Character Behavior Chart* on page 13.

4. The students can share their thoughts with either the whole group or a small group of students.

5. Ask the students to again refer to the *Criminal Behavior Chart* and the *Misdemeanors and Felonies* descriptions on pages 10 - 13. Ask them to decide whether any of the unacceptable behaviors they listed for the characters in the tale are criminal.

6. Ask the class, *"Do you think there was a crime committed by any character in the fairy tale?"* Ask, *"What crime might it be?"*

7. Guide the class in deciding upon the crime from the descriptions on pages 10-12.

8. Now the class can prepare for the trial if they determine they should do so. The class acts as the grand jury when the students decide to indict a character and bring him to trial.

9. You may wish to begin with *Little Red Riding Hood* which is developed as a case study. By beginning with this case you and your students can review the entire process to see if you followed the trial preparation, the order of the trial itself and completed the roles appropriately.

SESSION THREE:

PREPARE FOR THE TRIAL

1. Copy the PRETRIAL CLASS DISCUSSION QUESTIONS page for the fairy tale. Discuss the issues raised.

2. Copy and review the *"Students' Roles: What You Will Do"* on pages 15 and 16 so that the students understand what each person's role is in the trial.

3. Draw names from a box.

        Choose: 3 defense lawyers
                      3 prosecution lawyers
                      2 bailiffs
                      2 judges
                      2 witnesses or more for the prosecution
                      2 witnesses or more for the defense

4. All of the students should have a role in preparing for the trial. Students whose names were not chosen from the box will act as paralegals, writing questions and doing research for the lawyers.

5. The JURY may be another class, even a class at an upper grade level. When the trial is scheduled, ask the jury's teacher to go over the class' role, their responsibilities and what is expected of them prior to the trial. Have the teacher distribute to the jury *"The Jury's Job: Jury Deliberation"* (p. 20), *"The Juror Decision Page"* (p. 21), and *"Jury Foreman's Job"* (p. 22).

6. Defense and prosecution lawyers will write their legal arguments and their opening and closing statements. Copy the *Legal Argument Form* (p. 24) and the *Opening* (p. 23) and *Closing* (p. 25) *Statement Forms* into a Student Packet for the lawyers. Please note that these students may need more time and some guidance to do their work for the case.

7. Draw the names of students who will develop the questions for the witnesses, for the prosecution and defense lawyers. When they are finished, the lawyers should go over these questions. You may help them to shape their questions if necessary. All students may contribute their questions to this effort by writing them at the bottom of the <u>Pretrial Discussion Questions</u> page for the case.

PUTTING IT ALL TOGETHER

The Day Before the Mock Trial

1. Review *"The Trial Procedure"* (p. 17) with your students.

2. Ask the jury's teacher to review this procedure before the trial and inform students they will have to be perfectly quiet during the trial, listening for evidence.

3. The lawyers and the witnesses should run through the trial, paying attention to their dramatization skills: voice, expression, body language, and gestures. They will be following the order of the trial.

4. Other students may listen quietly, unless they have other jobs to complete for the trial.

5. Behavior is extremely important during practice and the trial itself. QUIET is the rule.

<u>Student Information Packet</u>
Criminal Behavior Chart
Character Behavior Chart
Students' Roles
The Trial Procedure
Glossary of Legal Terms

<u>Jury Packet</u>
The Jury's Job: Jury Deliberation
The Juror Decision Page
Jury Foreman's Job

<u>Lawyer Packet</u>
Opening Statement Form
Legal Argument Form
Closing Statement Form

<u>Individual Fairy Tale Trial Packets</u>
Information Page
Pretrial Discussion Questions
Post Trial Discussion Questions

TO THE STUDENT: CRIMINAL BEHAVIOR CHART

There are many types of wrongdoings. Not all wrongdoings are crimes. For example, it is wrong to slap or push someone, but these actions are not crimes.

A **felony**, a serious crime punishable by fine, imprisonment, and other punishments, is usually considered as one of four levels of crime. Each state lists felonies in Level 1, 2, 3, or 4 or Level A, B, C, or D. The more serious the felony, the more severe is the punishment. In most states if a crime is not a felony, it is called a **misdemeanor**, which is a less serious crime than a felony and is usually punishable by a fine. The following examples will show you how misdemeanors and felonies are grouped or classified.

In most states punishments vary with each case. Judges consider the person's history, any past crimes, the type of crime committed, etc., before deciding on a sentence. When a person is found guilty of a crime, the punishment must fit the crime. The judge, and in some cases the jury, will look at the local, state, or federal statutes which define the crime and its possible punishments. The judge has several choices for punishments: parole, community service, fines, and imprisonment.

Parole is the conditional release of a prisoner from his sentence. The parolee must follow certain instructions during the time of his parole.

Community service is a sentence of unpaid work performed somewhere in the local community, such as a library, a forest or park land, etc.

Fines are fees or money a criminal must pay to make "restitution" or payback for something stolen or damaged.

Imprisonment is time that a criminal must spend in jail as punishment for his crime.

The following chart lists some of the crimes and their possible sentences. These crimes are commonly found in fairy tales. The sentences vary depending on the value, for example, of something that is robbed, whether a defendant has committed any crimes before, and many other factors. Use the chart as reference as you work through a fairy tale and a fairy tale trial.

CRIMINAL BEHAVIOR CHART

MISDEMEANORS

PUNISHMENT

CLASS 1 MISDEMEANORS

Contributing to dependency or neglect of a child - causing neglect of a child who is in one's legal custody	Fines; imprisonment
Criminal Trespass - to enter someone's property without permission	Fines; imprisonment
Computer Trespass - to use or to get information from another person's computer without permission	Fines; imprisonment
Aggravated Assault - to threaten, to use a knife or gun	Fines; imprisonment
Fraud - to mislead or to fool someone into believing that he will be paid (bad check/charge)	Fines; payback; imprisonment
Criminal Damage to Property - to knowingly damage someone's property	Fines; payback; imprisonment
Theft - to take someone's property worth less than $300, with no use of threat	Fines; payback; imprisonment

CLASS 2 MISDEMEANORS

PUNISHMENT

Battery - to touch someone in a rude or angry way	Fines; imprisonment
Obstructing (blocking) Traffic - to block vehicle or pedestrian traffic	Fines; imprisonment

CLASS 3 MISDEMEANORS

PUNISHMENT

Assault - to threaten to harm another person	Fines; imprisonment

FELONIES

CLASS 1 FELONIES

PUNISHMENT

Armed Robbery with Injury - to take someone's property while holding a knife or a gun and to cause serious injury to someone	Fines; payback; 4-15 years' imprisonment
Armed Burglary with Injury - to break into and enter someone's home while armed with a gun or knife and to cause serious injury to that person	Fines; payback; 4-15 years' imprisonment
Murder - to kill another person	Varies from 20-40 years to life in prison to death
Conspiracy and Attempted Murder - to plot or to plan and to try to kill a person	Varies from 20-40 years to life in prison to death

CLASS 2 FELONIES	PUNISHMENT
Aggravated Battery - to injure a person to the point of risking his death or to cause him/her serious permanent injury	3 - 7 years' imprisonment
Armed Robbery - to take someone's property while armed (holding) with a knife or a gun	3 - 7 years' imprisonment
Car jacking - to take someone's car by force	3 - 7 years' imprisonment
Armed Burglary - to break into and enter someone's home while armed with a gun or a knife	3 - 7 years' imprisonment
Child Abduction - to take someone else's child	3 - 7 years' imprisonment
Kidnaping - (*and Attempted*) to hide (secretly or by force or threat of force) and to keep someone against his will	3 - 7 years' imprisonment
Confinement Against One's Will - to hold someone against his wishes	3 - 7 years' imprisonment
Forcible Detention - to force someone to stay somewhere he doesn't want to be	3 - 7 years' imprisonment
Fraud - to carry out a plan to deceive or trick another person, which results in the loss of money or something valuable	3 - 7 years' imprisonment
Bribery - to offer or to accept a valuable gift in order to influence or change a decision that is important to the public	3 - 7 years' imprisonment

CLASS 3 FELONIES	PUNISHMENT
Theft - to take someone's property worth more than $300, no threat	2 - 5 years' imprisonment
Robbery - to knowingly take property from another person, use threat	2 - 5 years' imprisonment
Burglary - to break into and enter a person's home intending to rob	2 - 5 years' imprisonment
Retail Theft - to take property worth more than $150 from a merchant/ store	2 - 5 years' imprisonment

CLASS 4 FELONIES	PUNISHMENT
Child abandonment - leaving a child under the age of fourteen without parental or appropriate care	1 - 3 years' imprisonment
Criminal Trespass - to break into and enter someone's home or a public building where known not to be welcome; or to physically do something to someone's property	1 - 3 years' imprisonment
Cruelty to children - the act of a person exposing a child in his legal authority to danger through exposure to severe weather or any other way that would injure his health; an act relating to inappropriate supervision of a child	1 - 3 years' imprisonment
Unlawful Restraint - to detain or to hold someone	1 - 3 years' imprisonment
Retail theft - to take property worth less than $150 from a merchant or store	1 - 3 years' imprisonment
Criminal Damage to Property - to knowingly damage someone's property valued at more than $300	1 - 3 years' imprisonment

CHARACTER BEHAVIOR CHART

BEHAVIORS

Character in the Story:	Acceptable/Good	Unacceptable/Not Good
_____ _____ _____ _____ _____ _____	Behavior:_____ Reason_____ Behavior:_____ Reason_____ Behavior:_____ Reason_____ Behavior:_____ Reason_____ Behavior:_____ Reason_____ Behavior:_____ Reason_____ Behavior:_____ Reason_____	Behavior:_____ Reason_____ Behavior:_____ Reason_____ Behavior:_____ Reason_____ Behavior:_____ Reason_____ Behavior:_____ Reason_____ Behavior:_____ Reason_____ Behavior:_____ Reason_____

Each student is going to be an important part of a trial. A student may be one of the lawyers, a judge, a bailiff, a witness or the defendant. Others may be asked to help write questions for the witnesses. Review each of the roles with the students so that they all understand their roles.

defendant - fairy tale character who is accused of breaking a law.

defense lawyer or lawyers - those lawyers who will argue to support or defend the defendant (the accused). They will try to prove that the defendant is not guilty of the crime.

prosecution lawyer or lawyers - those lawyers who will charge a person with a crime and argue that he is guilty of that crime. They will try to prove that the defendant is guilty of the crime.

witness - fairy tale character who is summoned to the court and asked questions for the defense or prosecution of the case.

judge - an officer of the court who presides or rules over the court, making decisions about the law and the case during a trial.

bailiff - an officer of the court who keeps order, calls witnesses to the stand, and assists the judge in this manner.

grand jury - a group chosen by the court who must decide whether or not there is enough evidence to show that a crime was committed and to indict (accuse) someone of that crime. (Optional)

trial jury - a group of people (living in the area of a court) who must listen to all of the evidence in a trial and decide whether the defendant is guilty or not guilty.

The class must decide if there was a crime committed in the fairy tale. The class will act as the Grand Jury in each case to make this decision. If it is determined that a fairy tale character has committed a crime(s), the character will be indicted or accused of the crime(s) and the case will go to a Jury Trial. Students will assume their roles in putting the case together with all of the members of the class.

STUDENTS' ROLES:

WHAT YOU WILL DO

Find your role and read what your job responsibilities will be.

<u>defendant</u> - You are accused of a crime. You have been summoned to court for a trial. You have a lawyer defending you who will try to prove that you are not guilty. A prosecuting lawyer is trying to prove that you are guilty of the crime. You will work with your lawyer(s) to help him or her build a case to defend you. You may need to testify (be called to the witness stand and answer questions).

<u>defense lawyers(s) or public defender</u> - Your job is to build a case of evidence to prove that the defendant is not guilty. You will need to write an opening statement, a legal argument, and a closing statement. You will need to go back to the fairy tale to find reasons and proof (evidence) why the defendant is not guilty. Ask the teacher to assign several (4 or 5) students to help write questions for the witnesses you will call to the witness stand. You will need to give a list of witnesses to the bailiff. When all of this is done, you will be ready for the trial.

<u>prosecution lawyer(s)</u> - Your job is to prove that the accused (the defendant) is guilty as charged for the crime or crimes for which he or she is accused. You will write an opening statement, a legal argument, and a closing statement for the case, going into the fairy tale as needed for evidence. You will be given the *Opening* and *Closing Statements* and the *Legal Argument Form.* Ask the teacher to allow 4 or 5 students to help you write and compile questions for the witnesses you will question for the defense and the witnesses you will question for the prosecution. You will need to give a list of witnesses to the bailiff. When all of this work is done, you will be prepared to present the case to the judge and the jury.

<u>witness(es)</u> - You have been selected to dramatize or act out the role of a character in the fairy tale. You will be asked questions by all of the lawyers. You may dress up as the character, and remember to speak up and speak clearly.

<u>bailiff</u> - You are a uniformed officer assigned to the court room. Your job is to assist the judge and to keep order in the court room. You begin the trial by calling the court to order, saying:

*"PLEASE STAND. HEAR YE, HEAR YE. THE HONORABLE JUDGE _____
IS PRESIDING. COURT WILL NOW COME TO ORDER."*

You also call the witnesses for the prosecution and for the defense and
swear them in, saying:

*"RAISE YOUR RIGHT HAND AND REPEAT AFTER ME . . . 'I DO
SOLEMNLY SWEAR THAT ALL THE INFORMATION I AM ABOUT TO
TESTIFY IS THE TRUTH.' "*

<u>judge</u> - You are in charge of the courtroom and all of the cases that you hear. You advise
the jury and pronounce (give) the sentence to the defendant if he or she is found
guilty. You make the rules in your court room. You make decisions about how the law
is worked out in all of the cases you hear. You may ask the defendant and the witnesses questions. You may advise the jury or anyone involved in the case as a legal
advisor. You dismiss each case when it is finished.

<u>grand jury</u> - When a class has read a fairy tale and discussed the pretrial discussion ques-
tions, the class decides whether or nor there was a crime committed. The class is, at
that time, acting like the grand jury by making this decision and bringing or not bringing charges against a person and calling a trial.

<u>trial jury</u> - You are a member of the jury, also called the "petite" or little jury.
Your job is very important, as you are hearing all of the evidence in the
case. You will have to decide the defendant's future by voting guilty or
not guilty for each criminal act the defendant is accused of. See *"The Jury's
Job: Jury Deliberation"* for more details.

<u>jury foreman</u> - You have been
chosen as the spokesperson and
the leader of the jury. You will organize
the discussions and the voting of the members of the jury. Use the sheet called the
"Jury Foreman's Job."

THE TRIAL PROCEDURE

The bailiff opens the trial. *"Please Stand. Hear Ye, Hear Ye. The Honorable Judge _____ is presiding. Court will now come to order. This court is now in session. We will hear the case of _____ (the defendant), who is accused of _____. Would the defendant please stand?"*

THE ORDER OF THE TRIAL
   a. Opening Statements of the prosecution and the defense teams.
   b. Prosecution team calls and questions these witnesses.

1	4
2	5
3	6

   c. Defense team then cross-examines and questions those witnesses.
   d. The defense team calls any additional witnesses.

1	4
2	5
3	6

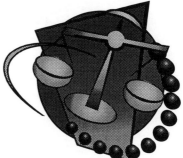

   e. The prosecution then cross-examines these witnesses.
   f. The prosecution and the defense teams each give their Closing Statements to the jury.
   g. The lawyers, the defendant, and the witnesses leave the room so that the jury can do its work.
   h. All return to the courtroom and come together to hear the verdict and the sentence. The jury foreman reads the verdict as the defendant stands. The judge gives the sentence if the defendant is guilty. The judge dismisses the jury and the case is then over.
   i. Use the Post Trial Discussion Questions after the trial to reflect on the trial experience.

THE JUDGE'S ROLE

1. The judge really holds the whole trial together. A strong leader or the teacher should take this role.

2. The judge follows the order of the trial exactly as required by law.

3. The judge leads the rest of the "actors" to follow the sequence of the trial.

4. The judge calls for the Opening Statements of the prosecution and the defense teams.

5. The judge asks the prosecution team to call and question their witnesses and the defense team to cross-examine (question) these witnesses.

6. The judge asks the defense team to call and question additional witnesses and the prosecution team to cross-examine these witnesses.

7. The judge directs the legal teams to give their Closing Statements.

8. The judge directs the jury to deliberate and to reach a verdict and advises them.

9. After a verdict is decided, the judge pronounces sentence on the defendant if he is found guilty. He closes the case if the defendant is found not guilty.

TO THE TEACHER:

JURY DELIBERATION

1. The teacher and the judge explain the importance of the case at hand and the decision and the consequences of the decision which they will have to make at the conclusion of the trial.

2. Draw a name from your class list to act as the Jury Foreman. Explain to the jury and to the foreman that the foreman is like the discussion leader or manager of the jury. Give the *"Jury Foreman's Job"* (p. 22) and the *"The Judge's Role"* (p. 18) to these two key players.

3. Distribute and review *"The Jury's Job: Jury Deliberation"* (p. 20), *"The Trial Procedure"* (p.17), *"The Juror Decision Page"* (p. 21), and the *"Jury Foreman's Job"* (p. 22) with the class before the trial. *"The Juror Decision Page"* may be used by each juror to help the student analyze the facts presented in the case.

4. Determine the rules. You may think the case should be decided with a simple majority vote. If you expect the jury to have a unanimous vote, be prepared for a lot more introspection and debate among the jurors. A trial is more intense and exciting when a unanimous vote is expected, but it does take a bit more time for the deliberation process.

5. The jury must try its best to come to a unanimous agreement on their verdict (vote). If they do not do so, the trial has a hung jury and the case has to go to trial again with a new jury.

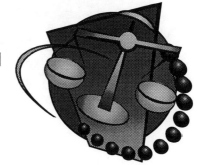

6. The jury discusses and deliberates until they have a verdict. At that time the defendant, lawyers, and witnesses return to the classroom for the jury's verdict and the judge's sentence.

7. After the verdict is read the sentence is given for the crime, the class discusses the importance of the case, what they have learned, and how it relates to their lives. Discussion and journaling are good ways for the students to reflect on this experience.

THE JURY'S JOB:
JURY DELIBERATION

1. Each member of the jury is responsible for thinking for himself.

2. A jury member must think clearly, ask questions, come to a conclusion and know why he believes as he does.

3. The jury sits in a circle facing each other. When the jury foreman polls the jury, each jury member gives his vote. If asked, he gives his reasons for his vote.

4. The jury must work well together, listening to each other and taking turns discussing the case with each other.

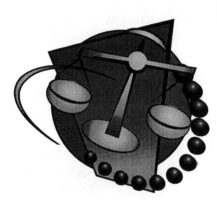

5. The jury discusses and each person tries to convince each other how to vote until they reach a UNANIMOUS (ALL AGREE) decision. Hopefully, the jury can decide on one verdict. If not, the case goes to court again to be heard by another jury. The jury members must work hard to convince other members to vote one way or the other.

6. Once the jury has reached a decision, everyone returns to the classroom. The judge asks the jury if they have reached a verdict. If so, the jury foreman reads the verdict while the defendant stands.

7. If the verdict is *not guilty*, the defendant is free to go and the case is closed. If the verdict is *guilty*, the defendant is then given a sentence by the judge.

THE JUROR DECISION PAGE

Defendant:

Charge:

Evidence Presented:

Witnesses:

NO	Witness Name	Information
1		
2		
3		
4		
5		
6		
7		
8		
9		
10		

Sort information and evidence under guilty and not guilty in the chart below.

GUILTY	NOT GUILTY

My conclusion is that the defendant _____ is _____ (guilty or not guilty) as charged. Circle the evidence that helped you make this decision and be prepared to explain your position.

JURY FOREMAN'S JOB

1. The jury foreman is appointed. The teacher can help a jury member draw a name for this job.

2. The jury sits in a circle facing each other. The jury foreman polls the jury aloud to take an initial vote.

"Who thinks _____ is guilty of _____?"
He takes a vote and writes down the vote.
"Who believes that _____ is NOT guilty of _____?"
The foreman counts the vote and writes it down.

3. The foreman asks each member of the jury to explain his vote.

He says, *"Let's start with you and go around the circle. Tell us how you voted and why."* (A member of the jury might begin like this. *"I believe that _____ is not guilty of _____ because . . ."*)
Each member of the jury explains his position. The jury foreman gives his vote and his opinion, too.

4. The jury continues to discuss the case. Some jury members will change their minds.

5. The jury foreman reminds the jury that **THE VERDICT MUST BE GUILTY OR NOT GUILTY WITH A UNANIMOUS (ALL AGREE) DECISION. IF THEY DO NOT AGREE, THE CASE WILL BE RETRIED**. The judge and the jury foreman discourage the jury from a "hung" vote.

6. The jury deliberates until they are again polled and reach a final decision, or verdict. When a final verdict is reached, the legal teams and the witnesses return to the classroom.

7. The judge asks the jury if they have a verdict. The jury foreman says, *"Yes, Your Honor, we have."*

8. The judge asks the defendant to stand while the jury foreman reads the verdict. Then the judge pronounces his sentence. The case is over.

 **O**PENING STATEMENT FORM

Name _____ Legal Team _____

Ladies and gentlemen of the jury, the defendant, _____ , is
accused of _____ and _____ .

We will prove that the defendant, _____ , is
_____ (guilty or not guilty) of these crimes. We know that:

1. _____

_____

2. _____

_____

3. _____

_____

4. _____

_____

5. _____

_____

6. _____

_____

7. _____

_____

8. _____

_____

 **LEGAL ARGUMENT FORM**

Name _____

Legal Team (side)

_____

STAND: I believe that _____ is _____
(guilty or not guilty) of _____ and _____
because:

List facts and reasons from the story to support your stand:

1._____

_____

2._____

_____

3._____

_____

4._____

_____

5._____

_____

6._____

_____

7._____

_____

 # CLOSING STATEMENT

Name _____ Legal Team _____

Ladies and Gentlemen of the jury, we have shown you that the defendant
_____ is _____(guilty or not guilty) of
_____and _____.

The evidence shows that the defendant _____ is _____
because:

1._____

_____

2._____

_____

3._____

_____

4._____

_____

5._____

_____

6._____

_____

7._____

_____

You must find the defendant _____(guilty or not
guilty) as charged.

TO THE TEACHER:

INTRODUCTION TO THE FAIRY TALE CASES

Following the first case, *Red Riding Hood & Family Vs The Wolf,* there is a sample case study. Its purpose is to walk you through the case. It should be helpful to you as you review your performance on your first case. For these reasons, you may wish to begin with *The Story of Little Red Riding Hood* so that you can review your case preparation and trial alongside the case study provided.

Please choose the fairy tales that are most appropriate for your students' ages and sophistication. *Little Red Riding Hood* would not be as difficult a case as *The Tinder Box* or *Toads and Diamonds.*

Information to read to the students:

As you read the following news releases, interviews, and other introductions to a possible "case," it is up to you to "read between the lines." You must look for possible wrongdoings as well as facts and evidence to support your thoughts.

Then read the entire fairy tale before you come to any conclusions about a character's actions.

If you have facts which support your class' (acting as the grand jury) decision to accuse a character of a crime or crimes, then it's time to proceed with a trial. Refer to all of the information in the Students' Packets in preparing for a trial.

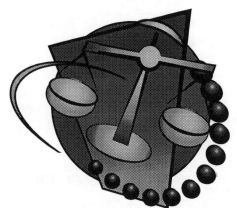

Please add to the questions listed as you discuss the Pretrial and Post Trial Discussion Questions. Most importantly, reflect on what you learn from each case and determine how it relates to your life.

Little Red Riding Hood

LOCKS KEEP YOUR HOME
SAFE AND SECURE
CALL 351-LOCKS

Hi! This is Jake, the Locksmith. I just fixed up Little Red Riding Hood's house with locks on all of the doors and windows. Boy, did she need those locks!

Did you hear what happened to her Grandma? Well, she was sick in bed and left the front door unlatched so that her granddaughter, Little Red Riding Hood, could get in by herself. Well, she really learned a sad lesson. Red Riding Hood had met a Wolf as she walked through the woods on the way to her grandmother's house that day. Unfortunately she told the Wolf where she was going, and he went ahead of her to Grandma's house and pretended he was Red Riding Hood, attacked her grandmother and ate her up! When Red Riding Hood arrived at her grandmother's house, the Wolf was disguised as Grandma. He was just about to eat her up, when a woodcutter saved her life.

Now you know why everyone should secure all of their doors and windows with the best locks available. I've been called by all of Red Riding Hood's neighbors to "lock up" their homes, too. They are very sad for Red Riding Hood and her family and don't ever want to see or hear of any violence in their neighborhood ever again.

**Don't you make the same mistake
that Grandma did.
Secure your home with my BEST locks.
Just call Jake at 351-LOCKS.**

PRETRIAL DISCUSSION QUESTIONS

What mistake did Little Red Riding Hood make?

How did this mistake contribute to her grandmother's murder?

Study the Criminal Behavior Chart. What crimes should the Wolf be accused of?

Are Little Red Riding Hood and her family justified in charging the Wolf with criminal trespass, assault, and murder?

What motivated the Wolf to eat the grandmother?

What might you say in defense of the Wolf?

Are there sufficient facts in this case to take this to a jury trial?

Do you as a class, acting as the Grand Jury, feel justified to recommend this case go to trial by jury?

WHAT QUESTIONS WOULD YOU LIKE TO ASK LITTLE RED RIDING HOOD, HER MOTHER, HER GRANDMOTHER, THE WOLF, OR THE WOODCUTTER?

A question for _____

The question: _____

A question for _____

The question: _____

A question for _____

The question: _____

POST TRIAL QUESTIONS

What were the criminal charges against the Wolf?

Examine the strategies of the defense team and discuss how they defended the accused Wolf.

Discuss the facts and strategies employed by the prosecution team.

Was there a verdict?

Do you agree with the verdict? Discuss.

If you were Little Red Riding Hood, how would you rewrite this story to avoid Grandma's murder?

What mistakes in judgement did the characters make?

If you were Little Red Riding Hood, would you have talked to the Wolf? Why or why not?

What lessons can be learned from this story?

How can you watch your actions in order to be safe when walking from home to another destination?

What other issues or ideas would you like to discuss about this case?

_____

_____

_____

_____

_____

SAMPLE CASE STUDY

Little Red Riding Hood & Family Vs The Wolf

PUTTING IT TOGETHER . . .

Let's look to see how this case should come together.

You read the story with a "critical eye," watching the characters' behaviors carefully. You saw that the Wolf, did in fact, enter Grandmother's house and ate up the grandmother.

You searched the Criminal Behavior Chart and the Glossary to determine whether or not these were criminal behaviors, verifying that the Wolf will be indicted (charged) with criminal trespass, assault, and murder.

Criminal trespass is defined as entering another's property without permission, a Class One Misdemeanor. The Wolf clearly did that as he tricked the grandmother and entered her house.

Assault is the act of threatening to harm another person. Clearly the grandmother was threatened by the Wolf. This is a Class Three Misdemeanor.

Murder is the act of killing another person. The Wolf committed this Class One Felony when he devoured the grandmother.

Based on the evidence in the story and your assessment of the Wolf's criminal behaviors, you proceeded to act as the Grand Jury. A trial was recommended.

Your classroom teacher assigned jobs for each of you: witness, judge, lawyer, bailiff, defendant, jury (another class), etc. The prosecution and defense teams had to "build" their cases with facts, evidence and strategy, creating opening and closing statements, legal arguments, and a list of necessary witnesses to question. Some of you wrote the questions for the witnesses. Prosecuting lawyers had to compile the evidence and reasons to prove that the Wolf is guilty. The defense team had to try to defend the Wolf's actions. Perhaps the Wolf could say that he was invited into Grandma's house, that she became violent and that he defended himself. The defendant in this case is a tough one to defend. You had to be creative about the defense strategies and the questioning of the witnesses. For example, a clever defense lawyer might ask Little Red Riding Hood, *"Haven't you been taught NOT to speak to strangers?"* and *"Why did you, in fact, tell the Wolf where you were going, when you might have put yourself and your grandmother in danger?"* The bailiff compiled a list of witnesses to be called and practiced his speech to introduce the judge and to swear in the witnesses. The judge ran the courtroom, following the order of the trial.

The jury and their teacher studied and performed their roles and procedures for the Wolf's trial. They discussed and debated each charge of criminal trespass, assault, and murder. They had to stick to the facts and evidence presented by the lawyers and the witnesses. Members of the jury had to defend their ideas and persuade others to "buy into" their line of thinking. The Wolf's character and past history were discussed, and reasons for his actions were given to justify his behavior for those who believed the Wolf was not guilty. Others who believed that the Wolf knew better and was guilty as charged needed to persuade other jurors to their line of thinking. The jury foreman kept order, polled votes periodically, and led discussions. Some jurors changed their votes and the foreman had to poll votes several times during the deliberations.

Once the jury had a verdict, the foreman rose and read the verdict with both classes present. The judge pronounced the sentence if the Wolf was found guilty and dismissed the jury. A post trial discussion of the case followed.

You thought about your role and how well you did. You discussed any difficulties you encountered in the preparation and presentation of the trial, as well as the jury's deliberation. This discussion is invaluable before you proceed to another case. Application of trial jobs to occupations was discussed, as well as the importance and relevance of the case in our lives today.

You have used so many valuable reading, writing and thinking skills. You showed cooperation as you worked through the Wolf case. Congratulations on a job well done!

The Tinder Box
by Hans Christian Andersen

GET INFORMED

Exclusive Newsline Interview

"Good evening, this is Barbara Watts with *Newsline*. Tonight will be the new King's first interview since he took over the land and married his Princess. Is this a story of romance and determination to win the Princess' hand in marriage; or is this story one of violence, crime, and rule by fear? Perhaps tonight's exclusive interview with the King will shed some light on his rule and the sudden changes in the land.

Later in the broadcast we will hear from the ghosts of the witch and the ghosts of the former King and Queen.

"Good Evening, Your Majesty. There appears to be conflicting information about your sudden appearance and appointment as King, as well as your sudden marriage. How *DID* all of this happen?"

"Well, Barbara, I acquired some wealth, moved here to this fair land, met the Princess, fell in love, and married her. It's that simple."

"Your Majesty, how do you account for the violent take-over of the castle and its rule? The former King and Queen, as well as the judges and the council, were attacked by three humongous dogs, thrown into the air, and smashed to pieces, were they not?"

"Barbara, Barbara, Barbara, this is all nonsense. It never happened. Ask anyone in the land, and they will tell you the people revolted and demanded that I take over as King. The people are happy, and the land is at peace."

"Thank you, Your Highness. We certainly appreciate that you spoke with us tonight. We'll now hear from the ghosts of the Witch and the ghosts of the former King and Queen.

"Good evening, Witch. Please tell us how you know the King."

"He was such a handsome soldier! I trusted him with my money and my tinder box. He took it all and cut off my head! What a mistake I made trusting him with my fortune."

"Please tell me more about this tinder box."

"Its special powers appear when you rub it. A loyal dog appears and grants your wish. Oh, boo, hoo. If only he had returned my tinder box, the land would be at peace, and we'd all

be alive today . . . me, the real King and the real Queen!"

"Thank you, Witch. And now, Ghosts of the former King and Queen, please tell us your account of what happened."

"Barbara, this man and his magic dogs kidnaped my daughter from the castle on several occasions. Because of his actions, he was to be hung, until I granted his one last request. Well the rest is history. So many were killed by his attack dogs, including us."

"We didn't get to attend our own daughter's wedding! Maybe that was for the best, considering that she *HAD* to marry *Him*. Do you think the people really want him as their King? I think they were afraid for their own lives. They were forced into it, just as the Princess was forced into marrying Him!"

"I'm sorry, Your Highnesses, but our time is up. The former King and Queen are pressing charges of kidnaping and murder and the Witch has charged the soldier with theft and murder.

"Tune in tomorrow for more on this story. This is Barbara Watts for *Newsline*. Good night."

PRETRIAL DISCUSSION QUESTIONS

What motivated the Soldier to kill the Witch?

What other choices could the Soldier have made?

How did he spend the money?

What wishes did the Soldier make?

Were they good wishes? Why or why not?

What other wishes could he have made?

Will he likely be a good King? Why? Why not?

What facts in the story show that the Soldier did something wrong?

Do you agree that the Soldier committed murder, theft, and kidnaping?

Based on the facts, do you as a class (acting as the Grand Jury) have enough evidence to ask for a jury trial in either the case of the Witch Vs The Soldier or the King and Queen Vs The Soldier?

WHAT OTHER QUESTIONS CAN YOU THINK OF TO ASK THE SOLDIER, THE PRINCESS, THE WITCH, THE FORMER KING OR QUEEN?

A question for_____

The question:_____

A question for_____

The question:_____

A question for_____

The question:_____

POST TRIAL DISCUSSION QUESTIONS

What crimes was the Soldier tried for?

Do you think the soldier had planned (intended) to commit these crimes?

What do you believe drove the Soldier to commit these crimes?

What evidence did the prosecution and defense teams use to prove and disprove the charges against the Soldier?

Do you believe the people of the land were fooled by the Soldier, or do you believe that they truly wanted him to be their King?

Was there a verdict? Did you agree with it? Explain.

Have you ever had a truly difficult choice to make? Explain.

What can you learn from this case?

How can you apply or use what you have learned in your own life every day?

What mistakes did the Witch, the real King and the real Queen make?

What could each of them have done differently?

What other ideas would you like to discuss regarding this case?

_____

_____

_____

_____

_____

_____

Sleeping Beauty
based on the story by Perrault

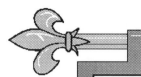
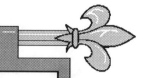

WANTED

BY OFFICIAL DECREE OF THE KING:

a handsome, loving prince is sought to break the evil spell of the evil Fairy

Only a handsome prince can break the spell placed on the lovely Princess. She has slept for one hundred years, as the evil Fairy predicted with her cursed spell. The prince must be strong and determined, as he will have to break through masses of thorny overgrown bushes and struggle up the old tower to where the Princess lies asleep.

The Prince must be determined to struggle against the difficulties he will face. He must be strong enough to climb the tower, and he must be ready to love, protect, and to marry the lovely Princess.

The Prince must be ready to accept that the Princess has only memories of the time of one hundred years ago. This may present problems in their marriage as she will have missed living for so many years.

The Prince may wish to capture the evil Fairy if he wants revenge or if the Princess wants revenge on the Fairy when she awakes. Charges would most likely be child abduction and/or confinement against one's will. The evil Fairy was last seen at the Princess' christening feast, where she placed the evil spell as an act of revenge for not having been invited to the celebration. It's been so long since the feast, that the Prince may indeed find it challenging to locate the evil Fairy.

Back to the matter at hand. First things first. The King and Queen offer generous rewards: riches, a castle, and best of all, the love of the beautiful Princess. Any Prince who possesses all of the above qualifications may contact the Palace at **1-800- IM-PRINCE** or by Internet at **www.prince@castle.com**.

PRETRIAL DISCUSSION QUESTIONS

Why wasn't the Fairy invited to the Princess' christening feast?

What circumstances made the Fairy angry and vengeful?

What spell did the evil Fairy place on the baby Princess?

How was the spell changed and why?

What purpose did the evil Fairy wish to accomplish by the spell?

Whom did the spell harm? How?

What other actions might the Fairy have considered instead of placing the evil spell on the Princess?

Did the evil Fairy commit a crime? If so, what crime(s)?

The Prince has charged the Fairy with child abduction and confinement against one's will, both felony charges. Does the class agree with these charges, and does the class find enough evidence to take this case to a jury? (The class acts as the Grand Jury by making this decision.)

WHAT QUESTIONS WOULD YOU LIKE TO ASK SLEEPING BEAUTY, THE PRINCE, THE ORIGINAL KING OR QUEEN, THE GOOD FAIRIES, THE EVIL FAIRY?

A question for _____

The question: _____

A question for _____

The question: _____

A question for _____

The question: _____

Post Trial Discussion Questions

What were the charges against the evil Fairy?

What is the difference between kidnaping and confinement against one's will?

How did the defense team use the facts to defend the Fairy?

In what ways were the prosecution lawyers skillful in their prosecution of the Fairy?

Was the Fairy found guilty as charged?

Discuss the jury's role in deciding on each charge. How did they do?

Have you every felt left out of a party, on the playground, or in any other situation? How does it feel in such a situation?

What might you try doing if you are left out?

Does revenge help you when someone hurts your feelings by leaving you out, not inviting you to a party, or refusing to play with you, etc.?

Can you learn anything from this case? Discuss.

What other ideas or concerns would you like to discuss about the case?

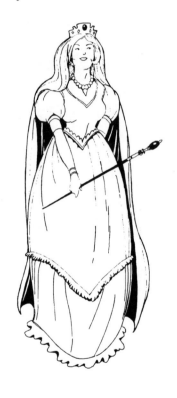

_____

_____

_____

_____

_____

Toads and Diamonds
adapted from the tale by Perrault

GET INFORMED

Fairy Warns Children to Be Kind to the Poor

An exclusive statement to the Toadally True Gazette

The Fairy released her statement today in order to protect more children from suffering the consequences of a bad tongue and poor manners. She encourages children and their parents to be helpful to those who are poor.

The Fairy revealed today to the Widow and to our reporter what actually happened to the Widow's two daughters at the Well.

When the younger and lovelier daughter walked far to fetch water, she encountered a poor woman (the Fairy disguised) who asked for a drink. The girl was kind and let her drink from the pitcher. The little girl was repaid by a good spell. From that day every time the girl spoke she would find a flower or a jewel coming from her mouth.

The older daughter, who looked so much like the Widow, was spoiled and unkind. The Widow sent her to the well to receive the same spell. When the elder daughter encountered the Fairy, the Fairy was dressed as a splendid lady. When the Fairy asked for a drink, the elder daughter was nasty and sarcastic. She begrudgingly offered the Fairy a drink. The Fairy placed a spell on the elder daughter so that when she spoke, toads or snakes would come from her mouth.

Subsequently the elder daughter was thrown out of her home by her mother, the Widow. The girl died in the woods because she could not take care of herself. The lovely sister ran away through the woods, but her fortune was good, since she met the Prince as she fled. They married and lived in the King's palace.

Meanwhile, charges of cruelty to children, neglect, child abandonment, and murder have been filed against the Widow by her lovely daughter, the new Princess. The Princess, too, warns all children to watch their words and manners and to be especially kind to those who are poor or need help.

PRETRIAL DISCUSSION QUESTIONS

Why do you think the mother, the Widow, favored her older daughter and treated the other so cruelly?

What behaviors do you admire in the younger daughter?

How did she treat the poor woman (Fairy)?

Was her spell a reward? How?

Why didn't the elder daughter know any manners?

What lesson could the elder daughter learn?

Do you think the Fairy was justified placing the two spells on the daughters? Why or why not?

Did the Widow do anything wrong? If so, what?

Is there enough evidence to bring charges against the Widow?

Do the facts in the case support the Princess' charges of cruelty to children, neglect, abandonment, and murder?

Does the class agree that the Widow's case should go to trial? (The class acts as the Grand Jury.)

WHAT OTHER QUESTIONS WOULD YOU LIKE TO ASK THE GIRLS, THE FAIRY, THE PRINCE, OR THE WIDOW?

A question for _____

The question: _____

A question for _____

The question: _____

POST TRIAL QUESTIONS

What was the Widow charged with?

How did the defense team support their case?

What facts and strategies did the prosecution team use?

Was there a verdict?

Do you agree with the verdict? Why? Why not?

Think about each character and what motivated each. Fill in the "T" chart below:

Character	Behavior
younger girl	goodness, kindness

Have you or someone you know acted selfishly or in an unkind way? Discuss.

How do you feel when you do a kind or generous act?

How do you feel when you are mean and selfish?

What messages or lessons can be learned from this story?

What other ideas about this story and the case would you like to discuss?

_____

_____

_____

The Bremen Town Musicians
adapted from the Brothers Grimm

RADIO NEWS FLASH

Just in from our news hotline is a report of dangerous home invaders. This report was phoned in by a band of robbers who reportedly fled their home outside the town of Bremen when the invaders crashed through their front window. The robbers, who later tried to reclaim their home, claim they were scratched, stabbed, and clubbed. They have not returned to their home. The band of robbers is pressing charges of criminal trespass, assault, and burglary. Just in …there are several people in the area reporting missing animals. Missing are an old donkey, a big hunting dog, a sad looking cat, and a rooster. They were seen traveling together on the road toward Bremen. If you see these animals, please call (888) R-A-D-I-O-B-R-E-M-E-N. We now return to our regularly scheduled broadcast . . .

POLICE REPORT

Police report they have found the missing animals in the house owned by the robbers. The animals were quite tired but well fed and in good condition. Police interrogated the animals for hours, as they were reluctant to share their true identities. They claimed they were town musicians. When questioned further, the animals told police why they had run away, how they had broken into the robbers' home, eaten their food, and scared off the robbers. They told police they had acted out of desperation, wanting the comfort and safety of a home and the delicious meal the robbers were eating. Later that night the cat scratched one of the robbers, who had returned to his house. The dog bit the robber's leg, and the donkey kicked him with his hoof. The animals' confessions were submitted to the Grand Jury with other evidence. The Grand Jury is considering the charges placed by the robbers.

In question is the fate of the animals, who each ran away to save his life. The fate of the robbers is undetermined. They currently live at a homeless shelter. Police are conducting background checks on the robbers to assess their activities in the Bremen area.

PRETRIAL DISCUSSION QUESTIONS

Why were the animals fleeing from their owners?

What were their plans?

Why did they change their plans?

What motivated the animals to invade the robbers' house?

What other choices might the animals have made?

What would you have done if you were one of the animals?

Do you agree with the robbers' charges against the animals?

Is there enough evidence in the story to back up the robbers' charges?

Does the class recommend that this case goes to a jury trial? (The class acts as the Grand Jury.)

WHAT OTHER QUESTIONS WOULD YOU LIKE TO ASK THE ANIMALS, THE ANIMALS' OWNERS, OR THE ROBBERS?

A question for _____

The question: _____

A question for _____

The question: _____

A question for _____

The question: _____

POST TRIAL DISCUSSION QUESTIONS

What wrongdoings were the animals accused of?

Did their actions break the law? How?

Why did the animals break into the robbers' house, eat their food, and scare them away? Were they justified in their actions?

Do you believe the animals acted appropriately when they scratched, bit, and kicked the returning robber? Explain.

In what other ways could the animals have created a home and found food for themselves?

What evidence and strategies did the defense team use to defend the animals?

How did the prosecution team put their case together? Discuss.

Do you agree with the outcome or verdict of the trial? Explain.

What lessons could be understood from this case?

How can you apply what you have learned to your own life?

What other ideas would you like to discuss about this case?

_____

_____

_____

_____

_____

The Hare and the Hedgehog
adapted from the tale by Grimm

GET INFORMED

A CONVERSATION WITH THE HARE'S FAMILY:
MRS. HARE, SUZIE HARE AND BILLY HARE AIRED ON HARENEWS LIVE.

"Good morning hares and other viewers. This is Diane Whiskers with the Harvey Hare family, who are grieving the death of Harvey Hare. Please tell us your story."

"We are distraught and beside ourselves with grief since my beloved husband dropped dead. We blame that Hedgehog who unfortunately shares our property and our cabbages. If it wasn't for him, our Harvey Hare would be alive today! Boo, hoo, boo, hoo, " wailed Mrs. Hare.

"That's right," said Suzie Hare. "That Hedge-hog challenged Dad to a race and tricked him into running seventy-four times. I couldn't see exactly what happened, but I heard the Hedge-hog say 'I am here already' 74 times. I don't understand it! My father was a speedy runner. He could beat the Hedge-hog any day. Besides, the Hedgehog's legs are crooked!"

"I suspect Mrs. Hedgehog of wrong doing. She must have been the one yelling 'I'm here already' seventy-four times. Dad tried seventy-four times to beat the hedgehog in the race, but he died. He should have won the first race. I think that Hedge-hog never even ran a race at all. He deceived my father, and now Dad is dead because of him!" yelled Billy.

"Thank you for sharing your story. I understand it must be very painful for you to tell this on national television. Is it true, Mrs. Hare, that you are charging the Hedgehog with fraud, murder, and theft?"

"Yes, Diane. The Grand Jury is considering the evidence at this time. We are hopeful that justice will prevail."

"Thank you, Mrs. Hare, Suzie and Billy.

"Tune in tomorrow to learn about the Grand Jury's decision in this case. This is Diane Whiskers for HARENEWS LIVE."

PRETRIAL DISCUSSION QUESTIONS

Why was the Hedgehog angry with the Hare?

Why did he challenge the Hare to a race?

Do you think the Hedgehog was stupid to do this? Why or why not?

Why did the Hare family suspect the Hedgehog of wrongdoing?

Did the Hedgehog do anything wrong?

Study the Criminal Behavior Chart. Did the Hedgehog commit any crimes? Explain.

What would have been a fair race for the Hare and the Hedgehog?

Is there enough evidence and are there sufficient facts to charge the Hedgehog with fraud, murder, and theft?

Does the class believe this case should go to a jury trial? (The class acts as the Grand Jury in this decision.)

WHAT QUESTIONS WOULD YOU LIKE TO ASK THE HEDGEHOG, HIS WIFE, OR THE HARE?

A question for_____

The question:_____

A question for_____

The question:_____

A question for_____

The question:_____

POST TRIAL DISCUSSION QUESTIONS

What were the charges against the Hedgehog?

Do you think they were justified?

Discuss the defense team's defense of the Hedgehog.

How well did the prosecution team do? Discuss facts and strategies they used.

Was there a verdict? Do you agree with the verdict and the sentence if there was one? Why or why not?

When the Hare made fun of the Hedgehog's legs, it appeared that he was prejudiced about the appearance, the ability and the swiftness of the Hedgehog. Discuss situations where you or someone you know was made fun of or harassed because of being different.

If you were rewriting this fairy tale, what would you change?

How accepting are you of others who are different in appearance and/or in their ways of thinking? Discuss.

What issues are presented in this case?

What have you learned, questioned, or thought about from this case?

What other issues would you care to discuss regarding this story and this case?

_____

_____

_____

_____

_____

Aladdin and the Wonderful Lamp
author unknown

It's a Case of Magic
A Dreadful Secret Threatens Aladdin
and His Princess

If money was the answer to everything, Aladdin had it all: a great palace, riches, the beautiful Princess as his wife. Then Aladdin's happy world seemed to fall apart.

As he returned from a hunting trip, he found his palace and his wife gone. The Sultan agreed to give Aladdin 40 days to find the Princess and bring her home or Aladdin would lose his head.

It really was a case of magic. The African magician who had pretended to be his uncle had returned for the magic lamp, his riches, and his Princess. Aladdin had long ago journeyed with the magician, retrieved the magic ring and the magic lamp, refusing to give the lamp to the magician.

Aladdin suspected the magician had returned. Aladdin rubbed the magic ring, asking the genie to take him to the Princess. Alas, when he was with his Princess, she told him how she had unknowingly traded the magic lamp for a new copper lamp. The magician had used the lamp to take possession of the palace and the Princess. Now the magician was insisting that she marry him.

Aladdin gave the Princess a poison to slip into the magician's wine, and the magician died quickly. After retrieving the magic lamp, the genie returned them and their palace home. All was well that ended well. Who would ever know it was a case of magic?

PRETRIAL DISCUSSION QUESTIONS

There were many twists and turns in this story. What were some of them?

Think about the magician's behaviors. Did he do anything wrong?

Examine the Criminal Behavior Chart to see if the magician committed any crimes. If so, what crimes?

Do you believe the magician committed criminals acts of fraud, kidnaping, and conspiracy to murder?

Is there enough evidence to charge the magician with these crimes?

Now examine Aladdin's behaviors. Discuss possible wrongdoings.

Are any one these wrongdoings actual crimes?

Is there enough evidence in the story to charge Aladdin with robbery and murder?

Can the Princess be charged with murder also?

As a class, decide who should be charged and the specific charges to be placed.

Did the class find enough facts and supportive evidence to bring the case to a jury trial? (The class acts as the Grand Jury.)

WHAT QUESTIONS WOULD YOU LIKE TO ASK ALADDIN'S MOTHER, THE MAGICIAN, ALADDIN, THE SULTAN, OR THE PRINCESS?

A question for _____

The question: _____

A question for _____

The question: _____

POST TRIAL DISCUSSION QUESTIONS

Which trial did your class choose? What were the charges?

Discuss the magician's motivation to deceive Aladdin and his mother.

What were Aladdin's desires? Why did he take the lamp and continue to act as he did?

Examine the defense team's approach. Discuss.

How well did the prosecution team present their argument? Explain.

What evidence was brought forth?

Was there a verdict?

Do you agree with the verdict? Explain your thinking.

Compare and contrast the magician with Aladdin. Make a Venn diagram showing how they are alike and how they are different.

Does money buy happiness?

Is there anything wrong with the message of this interesting fairy tale? Discuss.

What other issues would you like to discuss about this story and this case?

_____

_____

_____

_____

The Gingerbread Boy
Author Unknown *

 # GET INFORMED

The Gingerbread Boy Tells His Story of His Life on the Run

I remember my first experiences. I recall being awfully hot. At last an old woman opened the oven door, and I began my life on the run. Because I looked so delicious, I was chased by the little old woman and the little old man and so many others. You just don't know what it's like being a fugitive!

I began to make a game of it. I actually liked the victory of escaping from so many people in so many different places.

I was even chased by a cow and a horse! I wasn't going to be owned by anybody, and I wasn't planning to ever be eaten. I had other plans for myself. Maybe I'd meet up with other Gingerbread people and have friends, travel, and see the world.

I was a happy gingerbread boy until I was outfoxed by . . . you guessed . . . a fox! I couldn't get wet, of course, and needed to cross the river to escape everyone who was still chasing me. The fox promised not to eat me. As I rode on his back across the river, the water became deeper and deeper. The fox suggested that I jump on his nose. Can you guess what happened next? Crumbs . . .

That was the end of my life and my freedom. All of my plans and dreams were gone with a few bites. Do you know what I learned? Never trust a fox!

Now you children watch out next time your mother or grandmother bakes gingerbread boys. Be careful opening that oven door!

*(There are many retold versions of this story. Use one with the fox crossing the river and the gingerbread boy on his back at the story's end.)

PRETRIAL DISCUSSION QUESTIONS

How was the gingerbread boy created?

What did he do to surprise the little old woman?

Who chased him?

Why did so many people and animals chase the gingerbread boy?

It seemed that the gingerbread boy enjoyed being chased. Why do you think he liked being chased?

Did the gingerbread boy have the right to his freedom? Discuss.

Why did the gingerbread boy trust the fox?

Was a crime committed by the fox? If so, what?

The little old man and the little old woman saw what happened. They have filed charges of fraud and murder against the fox. Do you agree with their charges?

Does the class agree that there is enough evidence to take this case to a jury trial? (The class acts as the Grand Jury with this decision.)

WHAT QUESTIONS WOULD YOU LIKE TO ASK THE GINGERBREAD BOY, THE LITTLE OLD MAN, THE LITTLE OLD WOMAN, THE PEOPLE AND/OR ANIMALS WHO CHASED HIM, OR THE FOX?

A question for _____

The question: _____

A question for _____

The question: _____

POST TRIAL DISCUSSION QUESTIONS

What were the charges against the fox?

How did the defense team defend the fox's actions?

What facts and ideas did the prosecution team use against the fox?

Was there a verdict?

Do you agree with the verdict? Why or why not?

What mistake did the gingerbread boy make?

Why did the gingerbread boy use poor judgement in the situation with the fox?

Have you ever been lost or tired or in a situation where you needed help? What did you do?

What would you have done if you were the gingerbread boy and you were on the run?

What lesson(s) in safety can you learn from this story?

What other ideas would you like to discuss about this story and this case?

_____

_____

_____

_____

_____

_____

The Pied Piper of Hamelin
adapted from the tale by Robert Browning

WANTED

The Pied Piper is wanted on charges of kidnapping all but one of the children from the town of Hamelin. He is strange looking in his long bright colored coat. He has sharp blue eyes and long blond hair. He wears a long tasseled cap and carries a horn resembling a long pipe. Further details follow.

The town of Hamelin was rescued from their rat problem by the Pied Piper, a stranger who offered to rid the town of its vermin. After the Pied Piper did as he promised, the Mayor and the council refused to pay the 1000 golden guilders they had promised the Pied Piper upon completion of the task.

The Pied Piper threatened the Mayor and the council. He used his powers by blowing sweet notes from the pipe horn. This time all of the children were mesmerized by the sounds of the horn and followed the Pied Piper out of town. They traveled to an unknown place as they walked through a passage in the mountainside. Only a lame child remained in Hamelin, as he walked too slowly to complete the journey with the other children.

The mayor and the council, for some time, offered rewards of silver and gold to the Pied Piper for his return of the town's children, but the Pied Piper and the children have not returned.

At this time the reward money will go to anyone who finds the Pied Piper and gets him to return to Hamelin with all of the town's children. Kidnapping charges have been filed against the Pied Piper. However, the Mayor and the council have discussed dropping or lessening the charges if all of the children are returned to Hamelin unharmed.

If you have seen the Pied Piper and the children of Hamelin, please call the MOST WANTED HOTLINE at 1-800-ICPIPER.

PRETRIAL DISCUSSION QUESTIONS

What problems did the town of Hamelin have?

Why didn't the Mayor do anything to solve the vermin problem?

What did the Pied Piper look like?

How did the townspeople react to him?

How did he offer to help the town of Hamelin?

What did he ask in return for ridding the town of rats?

Was an agreement made between the Mayor and council and the Pied Piper? What was that agreement?

Why did the Pied Piper threaten the Mayor and the townspeople?

(This could be another case: The Pied Piper could accuse the Mayor and the council of fraud.)

What is the Pied Piper accused of? Do you agree with the charges?

Does the class agree that there is sufficient evidence to bring the case against the Pied Piper to trial? (The class acts as the Grand Jury in making this decision.)

WHAT QUESTIONS WOULD YOU LIKE TO ASK THE RATS, THE CHILDREN, THE MAYOR, THE TOWNSPEOPLE, OR THE PIED PIPER?

A question for _____

The question: _____

A question for _____

The question: _____

POST TRIAL DISCUSSION QUESTIONS

What were the charges against the Pied Piper?

Evaluate the facts and the strategies the defense team used to defend the Pied Piper. Discuss.

How well did the prosecution team put forth their argument?

Was there a verdict?

Was there a sentence?

Do you agree with the verdict and the sentence? Why or why not?

How was the Pied Piper deceived (tricked) by the Mayor and the council?

When he wasn't paid the guilders promised to him, what could he have done instead of using threats and kidnaping the children?

Is it right to do something wrong when you are wronged? Discuss.

What would you have done if you were the Pied Piper and you weren't paid?

What lessons can you learn from this story?

What other concerns or issues would you like to discuss about this story and this case?

_____

_____

_____

_____

_____

Cinderella

A CONVERSATION WITH . . . CINDERELLA TELLS HER STORY

One day Queen Cynthia's great grandchildren were playing in the attic of the palace when Benjamin stumbled upon an old trunk. As he rummaged through its belongings, he found an old tattered dress and an apron, both with burn holes and ashes. To Benjamin's amazement, he found a delicate pair of glass slippers. Benjamin called his brother Andrew and sister Meredith to show them his newly found treasures.

The three great grandchildren visited their Great Grandmother, Queen Cynthia, and inquired about the trunk. *"Well, it's time I told you about my childhood,"* she said pensively as she leaned forward from her throne. "My mother died when I was quite young. After my father remarried, my stepmother treated me cruelly. I was forced to wash our floors, scrub the house, and clean the fireplace grates. I rested after my chores in the soot of the chimney and was called 'Cinderella.' Although my stepsisters were well cared for, I labored hard and slept on a straw mattress in the attic. Besides the physical work that I was coerced to do daily, I was constantly scorned, belittled, and laughed at by my stepmother and my stepsisters.

One evening after dressing and adorning my stepsisters for the Prince's Ball, my Fairy Godmother appeared, dressed me for the Ball, and off I went in a handsome carriage. I danced all night with the Prince, but ran from the palace at the stroke of midnight, dropping one of my glass slippers.

The Prince ordered all maidens to try on the glass slipper. To the surprise of my stepsisters and stepmother, my delicate foot fit perfectly. I was taken from a life of scorn and servitude to a royal life of splendor and happiness with my handsome Prince. We had so many good years together. The only difficulty we endured was the trial. The Prince insisted upon charging my stepmother and my father with neglect and cruelty to a child. Other than the court battle, my life has been blessed.

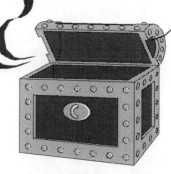

56

PRETRIAL DISCUSSION QUESTIONS

What major events changed Cinderella's life?

How were her mother's death and her father's remarriage difficult for Cinderella?

What was her family life like after her father remarried?

Why do you think the Stepmother treated Cinderella so badly?

Why do you think the Stepsisters were cruel to Cinderella?

Consider the behaviors of the characters and the charges placed by the Prince. Do you agree with these charges? Why?

Discuss the meaning of the charges and their consequences to the accused.

Is there enough evidence in the story to support the Prince's charges? Explain.

Does the class agree that Cinderella's Stepmother and her father's case should go to trial by jury? (The class acts as the Grand Jury in making this decision.)

WHAT QUESTIONS WOULD YOU LIKE TO ASK THE STEPMOTHER, STEPSISTERS, FATHER, CINDERELLA, FAIRY GODMOTHER, OR THE PRINCE?

A question for _____

The question: _____

A question for _____

The question: _____

A question for _____

The question: _____

POST TRIAL DISCUSSION QUESTIONS

What were the criminal charges against the Father and the Stepmother?

What strategies and evidence did the defense team use to defend the Stepmother and the Father?

Discuss the argument that the prosecution team used.

Was there a verdict? Discuss.

Do you agree that the Stepmother and the Father were guilty of the charges of neglect and cruelty to children?

Make a T chart to compare and contrast your life with Cinderella's childhood

Cinderella's Childhood	My Childhood

How is your life different from Cinderella's childhood?

How is your life better than Cinderella's childhood?

What important issues were brought up in this story and this case?

How should every child be treated? Reflect on this case and discuss what you have learned.

What other issues or ideas about this case would you like to discuss?

Two Bad Mice
adapted from the tale by Beatrice Potter

GET INFORMED

POLICE REPORT

Hunca Munca and Tom Thumb, husband and wife mice, were arrested on charges of criminal trespass, burglary, and criminal damage to property. The mice were apprehended after a thorough search of the home which housed the once lovely doll house. The parents of the Little Girl who owned the doll house called to report the damage and the items stolen. The dolls were too upset to be interviewed, however, photos of the crime scene were taken as evidence. The Little Girl was interviewed.

INTERVIEW WITH THE LITTLE GIRL

The Little Girl, whose name is withheld at this time, granted the police an interview about what she found when she returned to her room to play with her doll house and its belongings.

"What did you see when you returned home?" asked the policeman.

"The doll house was a total mess inside. Ceramic food was broken, clothing was dumped out of the window, feathers were plucked and flying everywhere, and several pieces of furniture were missing! A few chairs, some of my feathers and a cradle were missing. It was awful!

Those mice ought to be punished for what they did! They had no right even coming into the doll house uninvited! The nerve of them!" cried the Little Girl.

INSURANCE ASSESSOR'S REPORT

Damages reported and examined at the Little Girl's doll house included:

- a broken knife
- several pieces of smashed ceramic doll house foods
- a missing feather pillow
- two missing chairs
- a missing cradle
- missing doll clothes

PRETRIAL DISCUSSION QUESTIONS

Why did the mice enter the doll house?

Did they have permission to do so?

Why did they start breaking up the fake foods?

Do you believe they intended to wreck the doll house?

What might they have been thinking?

Study the Criminal Behavior Chart. Was there wrongdoing by the mice?

Are their behaviors considered crimes?

Based on the evidence in the story, does the class agree that Hunca Munca and Tom Thumb should stand trial for criminal trespass, burglary, and criminal damage to property? (The class acts as the Grand Jury by making this decision.)

WHAT QUESTIONS WOULD YOU LIKE TO ASK THE DOLLS, THE LITTLE GIRL, HER PARENTS, MUNCA, OR TOM THUMB?

A question for _____

The question: _____

A question for _____

The question: _____

A question for _____

The question: _____

POST TRIAL DISCUSSION QUESTIONS

What crimes were the mice charged with?

What facts and evidence did the defense team use to defend the mice? Discuss.

Discuss the prosecution's strategies and evidence used against the mice.

Do you think the mice were guilty as charged? Why or why not?

What lessons can we learn from this case?

Are there similar situations in real life that we can compare to this case? Discuss.

If you visited a friend's house and broke something at the friend's house, what responsibility do you have for the damage you caused?

Are you allowed to enter someone's house without their permission? Discuss this issue and its implications.

What choices might you make differently after working through this case? Explain.

What other questions would you like to discuss about this case?

_____

_____

_____

_____

_____

_____

_____

_____

GLOSSARY OF LEGAL TERMS

Accused - a. (verb) charged with; b. (noun) the defendant (person accused) in a criminal case.

Assault - the intent or plan to hurt another person or his property. Assault can be a threat of violence.

Attempted - the act of planning and plotting (i.e. to kidnap someone. This is treated as seriously as kidnaping and is a felony.)

Attempted murder and conspiracy to murder - the act of planning and /or trying to kill a person.

Battery - the act of physical contact or violent attack to a person.

Breaking and entering - the act of forcing open and/or entering private property without permission.

Burglary - the act of breaking into someone's house when he is not home or he is sleeping.

Child abandonment - leaving a child under the age of fourteen without parental or appropriate care.

Child abduction - the act of taking someone else's child.

Confinement against one's will - holding someone against his or her wishes.

Contributing to dependency or neglect of a child - causing neglect of a child who is in one's legal custody.

Crime - an act which violates or breaks the law.

Cross-examine - to question a witness after he or she has been questioned by the prosecuting lawyer or the defending lawyer.

Cruelty to children - act of a person exposing a child in his legal authority to danger through exposure to severe weather or any other way to injure his health; an act relating to inappropriate supervision of a child.

Defendant - a person who is accused of breaking the law.

Defense - an argument, usually by a lawyer, in support of a person accused of a crime.

Deliberate - to think about and talk with others to make a decision. A jury in a jury trial has the job of deliberating about a case.

Damage to property - (Criminal damage to property) - the act of knowingly ruining, damaging, or destroying another person's property. This is considered a misdemeanor, a less serious crime, unless the damage to property is $300 or more. Then the crime would be considered a felony, a more serious crime.

Evidence - data, information, facts and physical things that show or prove something happened.

Felony - a serious crime, such as murder or robbery. See the Criminal Behavior Chart for a listing of some common crimes and their possible sentences.

Forcible detention - the act of forcing someone to stay where he or she does not want to be.

Fraud - the act of carrying out a plan to deceive or trick another person, resulting in the loss of money or something valuable.

Grand jury - a group of people appointed to study the evidence in a case and to decide whether or not there is enough evidence to bring the case to trial.

Illegal - against the law or breaking the law.

Indict - to approve the act of charging a person with a crime and taking him or her to trial.

Indictment - a legal document prepared by the prosecuting attorney, stating the criminal charges against a defendant. An indictment must be approved by the grand jury in order to take the case to a jury trial.

Intent - a planned goal or purpose. A criminal may have the intent to commit a crime.

Judge - a person who deliberates and makes decisions in a court of law. A judge is an officer of the court and "manages" the court proceedings.

Jury - a group of persons who are appointed to hear a court case and to decide on a verdict.

Jury foreman - a person assigned by the jury to manage and direct the jury's discussions and deliberations.

Jury trial - a trial brought to court, in which the jury decides whether the defendant is guilty or not guilty as charged.

Kidnaping - the act of taking and holding someone against his will by force or threat of imminent force. In some states kidnaping is considered a capital crime, punishable by the death penalty.

Legal - something that is allowed or permitted by law.

Misdemeanor - an action that is against the law and less serious than a felony. See the Criminal Behavior Chart for a listing of common misdemeanors.

Murder - the act of killing another person. A planned murder is considered first degree murder.

Neglected or abused child - a minor (child under the age of 18) whose parent injures or creates a risk of injury which could cause the child's death; a child living in an environment which is harmful to his well-being.

Polling - to count votes. The jury foreman polls the jury several times during their deliberation process.

Prosecution - to take a person to court for a wrongdoing.

Questioning - the act of asking questions of witnesses during a trial.

Robbery - the taking of someone's possessions by threat of force or actual use of force.

Summons - a written legal note requiring someone to report to court as a juror or a witness.

Testify - to answer questions as a witness in a court of law.

Theft - to take someone's property worth more than $300, without threat or harm.

Trespassing (Criminal Trespass) - the act of entering another person's land with the idea of doing some violence or damage. Trespassing involves entering someone's property when not welcome there, changing or touching someone's land, or putting unwanted items on someone's property.

Verdict - the decision made by a jury at the end of a trial.

Witness - a person who testifies in court during a trial.

ASSESSMENT OF
STUDENT PERFORMANCE

Name _____ Date _____

Activity _____

Rate as follows: 4 limited understanding or grasp of skill/product

3 acceptable level of understanding or mastery of skill/product

2 commendable level of understanding or mastery of skill/product

1 exceptional understanding or mastery of skill/product

Assess only items which apply:

A. _____   Demonstrated critical reading skills.

B. _____   Demonstrated critical thinking skills.

C. _____   Demonstrated the ability to take a stand and support it with data.

D. _____   Showed understanding of behavior and laws which govern our society.

E. _____   Worked cooperatively as a legal team member or jury member.

F. _____   Wrote and presented a legal argument.

G. _____   Wrote effective questions for the witnesses.

H. _____   Demonstrated the ability to draw conclusions in this case as a lawyer or juror.

I. _____   Demonstrated the ability to dramatize the role of "lawyer" or "witness."

J. _____   Demonstrated the ability to convince others to accept a premise or position.

K. _____   Understands cause and effect of behaviors and consequences (fiction and real).